10/07

1X (12/07) 11/08   I

SERGEY BRIN
AND
LARRY PAGE
THE FOUNDERS OF Google™

INTERNET CAREER BIOGRAPHIES™

SERGEY BRIN
AND
LARRY PAGE

THE FOUNDERS OF Google™

CASEY WHITE

The Rosen Publishing Group, Inc., New York

Published in 2007 by The Rosen Publishing Group, Inc.
29 East 21st Street, New York, NY 10010

First Edition

Library of Congress Cataloging-in-Publication Data

White, Casey.
Sergey Brin and Larry Page: the founders of Google/
Casey White.—1st ed.
      p. cm.—(Internet career biographies)
Includes bibliographical references and index.
ISBN 1-4042-0716-3 (library binding)
1. Brin, Sergey, 1973– 2. Page, Larry, 1973–
3. Computer programmers—United States—Biography.
4. Internet programming—United States—Biography.
5. Google.
I. Title. II. Series.
QA76.2.B75W45 2006
005.10922—dc22

                                    2005031027

Printed in China

On the cover: Left to right: Larry Page and Sergey
Brin, the founders of Google.

CONTENTS

Since 1998, Sergey Brin and Larry Page, the two developers of the Internet search engine known as Google and founders of the company built around it, have rung up quite a series of accomplishments. According to the huge multinational accounting and financial services conglomerate Deloitte Touche Tohmatsu, in its first five years Google was the fastest-growing company ever. During that period, Google's revenue has increased by more than 400,000 percent.[1] In 2004, when Google became a publicly traded company, its initial public offering (IPO) of its stock was one of the most successful ever conducted. Needless to say, this success has made Brin and Page phenomenally wealthy individuals. They are the world's youngest (along with Bill Gates, founder of Microsoft) self-made billionaires, worth an estimated $7 to $10 billion each. The IPO also made instant millionaires of more than 1,000 Google employees who owned stock options.

Even more impressive is what Google has achieved in terms of what entrepreneurs and advertisers sometimes refer to as "mind share." Market share is the percentage of business a

Larry Page *(left)* and Sergey Brin pose for a rare portrait at the Google "campus" in Mountain View, California. Despite their massive wealth, the two are known for the relative simplicity of their lifestyles. Brin is seen here with one of his favorite modes of transportation, a Segway Human Transporter—an electric scooter admired as an environmentally sound alternative to both mass transportation and the automobile.

company or product controls in its marketplace. (Google controls 59 percent of the Internet search market.) Mind share, which is less easily quantifiable, is the degree of recognition, identification, and awareness that a company or product can claim in the minds of customers in that marketplace. Google's mind share is nothing less than phenomenal. Surveys consistently show Google as one of the companies most admired by the public.

More indicative of the company's place in the public consciousness, however, is the fact that the word "google," although perhaps not formally enshrined yet in most dictionaries as such, has entered the English language as a word with a meaning independent of the company that it identifies. "To google" is a verb meaning to seek information about a topic on the Internet. One presumably uses the Google search engine to engage in this activity, but not necessarily so. Google has become so identified with the activity for which it is used that "to google" has become the generally recognized term for that activity. This is the kind of mind share that entrepreneurs and advertisers dream about, an absolute triumph of what business marketing people call branding, or the art of achieving

Golfiat (Riese im
s (riesiger
chweiz. für

goodbye! [gʊt baɪ] (engl., »auf
Wiedersehen!«)
Good|will ['gʊt...], der; -s (engl.)
(Ansehen; Wohlwollen, freund-
liche Gesinnung; Firmen-,
Geschäftswert); **Good|will|rei|se**
goo|geln (im Internet, bes. in
Google suchen); ich goog[e]le;
Goo|gle ® ['gu:gl̩] *ohne Artikel*
(Internetsuchmaschine)
Gö|pel, der; -s, - (alte Drehvor-
richtung zum Antrieb von
Arbeitsmaschinen durch im

t für
= 100.

Google's "mind share" has become so pervasive worldwide that the name of the company has entered several languages, including English, as a verb. Seen here is an entry for the verb *googeln* in the 2004 edition of the leading German dictionary, *Duden*. Translated into English, the German word *googeln* means simply "to Google."

public recognition for a company's name, products, or logo. Few companies or products ever achieve this degree of recognition, one that allows them to enter common usage in the language as a generic term—one thinks of Kleenex, Xerox, and Coke.

Even more impressive, Brin and Page's company had managed to achieve this largely without advertising. As many a disappointed entrepreneur would be quick to testify, it is in fact not always enough to build a better mousetrap; advertising is often needed to inform consumers of its existence and convince them of its advantages as a product. Somehow, Brin and Page were able to achieve their success without spending a cent on advertising.

For the most part, the great success stories of American industry have been cases in which entrepreneurs have focused on a method of manufacturing, exploiting, or exchanging something tangible, for instance ships, trains, oil, soda, or electrical power.

But Google is quite different. It exploits something much less tangible: information. There are no factories producing "Googles" or Google products; no ships, planes, or trucks carry Googles to market. In fact, Google sells nothing at all to its millions of primary users. In the traditional sense, it produces nothing; a consumer never puts his or her hands on anything made by Google. It does its work in a mysterious realm of which most people are

Often dismissed as a quaint, hippie relic of the 1960s, lava lamps are a staple item of decoration at the Googleplex in Mountain View. They symbolize Google's nontraditional business practices.

profoundly aware yet still largely ignorant—
cyberspace.

What Google offers is perhaps the first and
most practical way to utilize the still largely
untapped potential of the personal computer and
the Internet to deliver information to individual
users. If, as has been written, we are currently
experiencing a shift in the epochs of human history from the Industrial Age to the Information
Age, the development of Google is surely destined to be remembered as a landmark event in
that transformation. Accordingly, in September
2005, *Vanity Fair* listed Brin and Page in first
place in their annual survey of the "most powerful leaders of the Information Age."[2] That year,
Google and the Internet portal Yahoo!, which
uses the Google search engine, took in more
advertising revenue than did the three major television networks during prime time. Alone,
Google took in more advertising revenue than
the nation's three most important newspapers—
the *New York Times*, the *Washington Post*, and
the *Wall Street Journal*.

What the personal computer, World Wide
Web, and Google (and other search engines like
it) offer the individual user is nothing less than

the ability to access, at any given moment, in a matter of seconds, from any location where a computer can be connected to an Internet hook-up, more information—more knowledge—than ever before possible in human history. (Each time a user conducts a search on Google, the Google search engine scrolls more than 8 billion Web pages, and it returns a result, on average, in half a second. Google conducts an estimated 100 million such searches every day.) Moreover, the amount of information accessible in this way increases every day.

Numerous observers have argued that the advent of the personal computer marks a development in human history as significant as the invention of the printing press in the fifteenth century. The organization of the World Wide Web as a means of utilizing the Internet increased the personal computer's potential exponentially; Google's ability to allow the individual user to access the information on the Web represents at least as important an innovation. This ability is literally transforming the way that individuals live.

CHAPTER ONE

"I Always Wanted to Go to Silicon Valley"

It probably could not have happened anywhere else, "it" being the particular combination of personalities, scientific and creative talent, educational opportunity, financial resources, vision, inventiveness, experimentation, and entrepreneurial culture that made Google possible. But in California's Silicon Valley in the late 1990s, stories like the one told today of Google's beginnings were fairly commonplace. There were dozens of would-be Googles around, dozens of brilliant young students and visionaries like Sergey Brin and Larry Page. It was what made the place so exciting, so cutting edge, for a certain type of person.

Described alternately as a "congeries of electronics firms"[1] and a "collection of characters and eccentrics,"[2] Silicon Valley is the geographical

The office complexes of high-tech companies glitter in the sunlight of the Silicon Valley community of Redwood Shores, California. Silicon Valley has more millionaires per capita than anywhere else in the United States, and it is the engine of the high-tech global economy.

region south of the San Francisco Bay stretching to the city of San Jose along and between Interstates 280 and 880, with the same approximate boundaries as Santa Clara County. It was formerly referred to as the Santa Clara Valley. Today that region is home to more than 4,000 high-tech industries, including some of the most recognizable companies—Apple, Yahoo!, Hewlett-Packard, Cisco, Adobe, Oracle, Sun, eBay, and, of course, Google—in the personal-computing and Internet fields.

A High-Tech Haven

Silicon Valley is a nickname for the region coined in 1972 by Don Hoefler, a journalist in the area who published his own newsletter covering the electronics industry. At the time, the valley was dominated by companies dedicated to the research and manufacture of semiconductors, which are an integral component of electronics devices and computers. Silicon is a common element found in clay, granite, quartz, and sand, which make up more than 25 percent of the earth's crust. Silicon is the principal component of semiconductors.

Tucked between two mountain ranges away from the Pacific coast, the Santa Clara Valley was one of the first regions of California settled by the Spanish. Prior to World War II (1939–1945), it was best known for its agriculture, famous for the orchards, farms, and ranches that produced carrots, almonds, tomatoes, prunes, apricots, plums, walnuts, peaches, pears, lemons, oranges, and avocados. Today, the city of San Jose prides itself as the high-tech capital of Silicon Valley, but on the eve of World War II, its economy was dependent on its being the fruit-canning capital of the world.

Today, those orchards are long gone. A number of developments brought about the region's transformation to Silicon Valley. During World War II, the U.S. Navy located one of its major research facilities in the area. A number of technology firms followed, taking advantage of navy contracts. Soon, the air force and National Aeronautics and Space Administration (NASA), the U.S. government agency responsible for outer space flight, also opened research labs there, and a number of private aerospace companies began doing business there as a result.

The primary stimulus in the creation of Silicon Valley, however, was the presence of Stanford University, in the city of Palo Alto.

Long known as the Harvard of the West, Stanford, with its world-class schools in engineering and the sciences, was an obvious source of high-tech talent. For years, however, most of its top graduates in engineering and the sciences would go east for work after graduation. This was because most of the nation's important engineering and technology firms were still located on the East Coast.

That began to change with the founding and development of Hewlett-Packard by William Hewlett and David Packard, former students in the Stanford engineering program. Located in Palo Alto, Hewlett-Packard was one of the first technology firms in the area that was not directly affiliated with or dependent on contracts from the navy or NASA.

Simultaneously, Stanford, with the vociferous encouragement of Frederick Terman, a professor in the engineering school, was taking active steps to encourage Stanford's talented graduates in the technology fields to remain and work in the region. Terman persuaded Stanford to convert some 700 acres (86 hectares) of unused land on its campus for use as an industrial park, where office and research and

An aerial view of Stanford University is pictured here. Frederick Terman (inset), the son of a Standford faculty member, was himself educated at Stanford and served there for years as a professor of electrical engineering and later as dean of the School of Engineering. Terman's belief in Stanford's potential as an incubator of high-tech industry was essential to the rise of Silicon Valley.

development space was rented out at low rates to innovative start-up technology companies. The first university-owned industrial park in the United States, the Stanford Research Park thus became the prototype for what are known today as technology incubators. The creation of the Stanford Research Park was followed by another Stanford initiative, the Honors Cooperative Program, also championed by Terman. The program allowed full-time employees of the technology companies in the area to pursue graduate degrees at Stanford on a part-time basis, with the companies paying the cost of tuition.

This nurturing environment for technology attracted even more top-flight talent to Stanford and to work in the region. No doubt the most important individual thus drawn to the region at this time was the world-famous physicist William Shockley. He was soon to win the Nobel Prize in Physics for his work in inventing the transistor. After breaking with Bell Labs over credit and compensation for the transistor, Shockley relocated to Mountain View, California, near Palo Alto, in large part because of the persistent lobbying of Terman. Terman promised to help Shockley find the brilliant talent he would need for his new

Incubating Technology

When Stanford University acted on Professor Frederick Terman's idea and created the Stanford Research Park in 1951, it was acting on an innovative proposition. Not only was the Stanford Research Park the first university-owned industrial park, but it was the first office park to be focused exclusively on high technology. As such, the Stanford Research Park can lay claim to being the nation's first technology incubator—an organization that provides the necessary resources, services, and support for a technology start-up in hopes of increasing its chances for survival and success.

Today, the 700 acres (86 ha) of the Stanford Research Park are home to 162 buildings that house more than 23,000 employees who work for 150 different companies in electronics, software, biotechnology, and other fields. Hewlett-Packard was among the first companies to take up space in the park, and today it remains a vital presence there. Among the other high-tech companies founded by Stanford graduates and professors through the Stanford Research Park are Cisco Systems, Sun Microsystems, and Yahoo!.

venture, the Shockley Semiconductor Laboratory. This would be the first research and manufacturing company in silicon devices in the soon-to-be-rechristened Silicon Valley. Shockley's new company failed to gain the success he envisioned, but his presence brought increased prestige and scientific credibility to the burgeoning high-tech region in the northern Santa Clara Valley. Although his reputation was later tarnished by strange behavior, bouts with mental illness, and the public avowal of bizarre racial theories, Shockley is remembered as the "man who brought silicon to Silicon Valley,"[3] and he and Terman are sometimes called the "fathers of Silicon Valley."[4]

THE INFORMATION AGE

High-tech firms such as Shockley's and its more successful offshoot, Fairchild Semiconductor, were soon followed in the valley by the venture capital firms with the resources and expertise to finance such risky start-up ventures. By the 1970s, the region's identity as Silicon Valley was firmly established, even as the focus of much of the brilliant young talent there was shifting toward the exciting new field of computing. In 1971, a firm in the valley, Intel, produced the first microprocessor chip, paving the way for the widespread production of the personal computer by another valley start-up, Apple. In 1980, the public got its first glimpse of the alliance between venture capital and high technology that was soon to remake the U.S. economy, when the initial public offering of stock in Apple sold out every share within minutes, making it the largest and most successful IPO since the Ford Motor Car Company went public in 1956.

If Ford was one of the most representative examples of the older American industrial example, Apple was the harbinger of the new Information Age, and it became emblematic of Silicon Valley. But even Apple was in some ways an industrial company, in the sense that it sold something—a computer—the consumer could put his or her hands on. Indeed, the design, or look, of Apple's products would ultimately become critical to its success. In August 1995, sixteen-month-old Silicon Valley start-up Netscape, the maker of a type of software known as a Web browser, raised almost $2 billion in its IPO, making it the biggest IPO in history to that date. It would soon be surpassed by others. The great age of Internet start-ups had begun.

MEETING WITH DESTINY

So what better place was there, in the late 1990s, for two young prodigies with an intense interest in computers to meet than in Silicon Valley? The first meeting actually took place in March 1995 during a tour of San Francisco that Stanford had arranged for prospective graduate students in computer science. Sergey Brin, who had already spent a year in the graduate program, was acting as a tour guide for the group. Larry Page, who had been accepted into the Stanford program but had not decided whether to accept, was making a weekend visit to the university and the surrounding region.

Perhaps because they were each accustomed to being the most brilliant young man in any group, they came away from this first meeting not particularly liking each other. Page thought the much more outgoing Brin was somewhat overbearing. "Sergey is pretty social; he likes meeting people," Page recalls, as if it should be obvious why that would conflict with his own notably more shy and reserved personality. "I thought he was pretty obnoxious. He had really strong opinions about things."[5]

The gregarious Brin was not much more impressed by Page, who despite his natural reticence admits that he was not particularly shy at that first meeting about expressing his own equally strong opinions. According to Google's official corporate history, "They argued about every topic they discussed."[6] "We both found each other obnoxious," Brin admits, but he maintains that there was an immediate connection of some sort as well. "But we say it a little bit jokingly. Obviously we spent a lot of time talking to each other, so there was something there. We had a kind of bantering thing going."[7]

But the two also obviously had a lot in common. They were born in the same year (1973), Page being five months older than Brin. Page was raised in Michigan. Brin, who was actually born in Moscow, in the then Soviet Union, grew up primarily in California and Maryland. Both were the sons of college professors. Page's father, Vincent, was a professor of computer science at Michigan State University in East Lansing. Mihail Brin fled the Soviet Union in 1979 with his family to escape a new round of anti-Semitism in that country. He was trained as a mathematician and economist and found work at the University of Maryland as a professor of economics.

Not surprising, Sergey and Larry grew up obsessed with math and with computers. Brin

A CAREER AND AN ADVENTURE

From the time of the famous gold strike at Sutter's Mill in 1849 and the gold rush that followed, California has been for Americans something of a promised land of opportunity, treasure, and adventure. In the early twentieth century, the centering of America's film industry there added an element of fantasy and mythmaking to that equation. One went to California to seek one's fortune—at first in the gold fields, later in the movies and in television.

By the 1990s, Silicon Valley was the place for young computer engineers to go to seek their fame and fortune, and in that context it seemed to offer these new seekers all the unfettered freedom and opportunity that California had earlier promised the gold rushers. In *The Nudist on the Late Shift and Other True Tales of Silicon Valley*, writer Po Bronson explains the appeal that Silicon Valley held for hyper-intelligent, restless would-be computer engineers and entrepreneurs such as Larry Page and Sergey Brin:

> Every generation that came before us had to make a choice in life between pursuing a steady career and pursuing wild adventures. In Silicon Valley, that trade-off has been recircuited. By injecting mind-boggling risk into the once stodgy domain of gray-suited business, young people no longer have to choose. It's a two-for-one deal: the career path has become an adventure into the unknown.

received his first computer at the age of nine as a birthday gift from his father; a short time later, he surprised one of his teachers by handing in a computer printout of his homework assignment. (This was still several years before computers would become commonplace items in homes.) Tremendously intelligent, he graduated from high school early and enrolled at the University of Maryland at the age of sixteen. By the time Page joined him at Stanford in September 1995, he was already in the second year of the doctoral program, although he found the California weather so good and his required course work so unstimulating, that he spent much of his time sailing, swimming, and diving.

ROLE MODEL, CAUTIONARY TALE

Page had advanced interests of his own at a young age. At the age of twelve, he read a biography of Nikola Tesla (1856–1943), the Serbian immigrant who went on to become one of the greatest scientists and inventors of the late nineteenth and early twentieth centuries. Tesla's life story inspired the young Page with the desire to invent something, but it also taught him a sadder, more practical lesson as well. As a young man,

The life of the brilliant Serbian-American scientist and inventor Nikola Tesla inspired Larry Page as both a positive and negative example. At one point hailed as the most original scientific mind of his day, Tesla ended his life in a morass of debt and insanity, a victim of sharp business practices and his own impracticality.

after coming to the United States, Tesla was cele-
brated as the world's greatest electrical engineer.
He was considered more brilliant even than his
former employer and great rival Thomas Edison
(1847–1931). Edison and Tesla had a bitter
falling-out after Edison reneged on a promise to
pay Tesla for several patents he developed for
Edison's company. (One of Tesla's greatest cham-
pions was his close friend and the great American
writer Mark Twain.)

Despite his innovative work with electricity
and radio, Tesla was never able to earn much
money for his work, and by middle age he was
deeply in debt and plagued by obsessive-compul-
sive disorder. He spent much of his last years
devising experimental methods with which he
attempted to contact Mars. He also worked on
what he characterized as a "death ray." At the
time of his lonely death at age eighty-six, he was
totally broke and remembered, if at all, as a
crackpot or mad scientist.

For Page, Tesla's sad life story was a cau-
tionary tale that taught him, even at his young
age, the dangers of not being practical about his
work. "Tesla had all these problems commer-
cializing his work," Page told writer John

Battelle in 2005. "I realized Tesla was the greatest inventor, but he didn't accomplish as much as he should have. I realized I wanted to invent things, but I also wanted to change the world. I wanted to get them out there, get them into people's hands so they can use them, because that's what really matters."[8]

Accordingly, Page arrived at Stanford, with a bachelor's degree in computer science from the University of Michigan, seemingly more focused than his new friend Brin. "I had decided I was either going to be a professor or start a company. I was really excited to get into Stanford. There wasn't any better place to go for that kind of aspiration. I always wanted to go to Silicon Valley."[9]

CHAPTER TWO

SEARCH, AND YOU SHALL FIND

B y the start of Page's second term at Stanford, in January 1996, he and Brin were working on a project together. Page had already gained some fame among the student body by building a working computer printer out of Legos, but he and Brin's new project was destined to have an even bigger impact.

He and Brin had become fascinated by the concept of "search." Although search was not considered a particularly cutting-edge topic of research in Silicon Valley, in a short time Page

This is the original storage cabinet assembled by Page and Brin to house the memory necessary to test their algorithm for the Google precursor. It consists of ten linked 4-gigabyte hard drives. The exterior is made, in part, from Legos, the popular children's toy—one of Page's favorite building materials.

and Brin were convinced that it held the key to practical use of the Internet.

In terms of personal computers and the Internet, "search" involves essentially what one would assume it does—the ability to look for, find, and access information on the Internet. What good, Page and Brin essentially asked themselves, is the wealth of information available on the Internet to the individual user unless there is a way of finding out what information is out there in cyberspace and how it can be accessed? Some people have suggested that search engines essentially serve as a card catalog to the Internet, in the way that a card catalog in a library serves as an index to all the books in that library. Without the card catalog, there would be no way of knowing whether or not that particular library had a particular book somewhere on its shelves. This is true unless a person physically examined every book on every shelf, looking for a particular title. Even if one had the time and patience to do so, this obviously is a very impractical and inefficient way to proceed.

Equally obvious is that one cannot roam the links, or library shelves, of the Internet in the same way that one peruses the shelves of a library. Most of the software developers in the valley were occupying themselves with how to create attractive and easy-to-use software that would allow users to access the Internet and to gain users (in what was sure to be a competitive field). Meanwhile, Page and Brin were concerning themselves with an even more fundamental question. Although, admittedly, the question did not really apply until a person had accessed the Internet: How could users find information once they were on the information superhighway?

THE PROBLEM WITH SEARCH ENGINES

Actually, Page more or less knew the answer to that question: use a search engine. Google would not be the first search engine; there were others already in existence. The conceptual premise and technology behind them were fine in some ways. Users could roam the Internet and search its billions of Web pages. Search engines more or less could tell the user what Web pages were out there on a particular subject, all in a matter of seconds.

The problem, as Page saw it, was with the quality of the information these early search engines returned. They were inefficient and arbitrary. This was in the sense that they did a very poor job in determining the quality of the information they found and distinguishing between sites. For example, one might get on the Internet hoping to find information about the woolly South American ruminant mammal known as the llama, type the word "llama" into the search box, and hit the search button. These early search engines would, in fact, return a long list of Web pages that had information about llamas. This was impressive, and one reason why everyone, in the late 1990s, seemed to be so excited about this thing called the Internet.

But Page saw a problem. As good as these engines might be at finding information, or "content," on the Internet about llamas, they were not particularly good at determining the quality of that information. They might provide the user with hundreds of listings of Web pages about llamas, but these listings, so far as the user could tell, were not in any particular order. There was no way for the user to tell, just by looking at the listings, which pages had the most information. The user could not tell which pages went into greater detail, or which was better for the user's purpose. To find that out, the user had to click on and actually read, or at least look at, the sites. This was time-consuming for the user, and from Page's perspective, inefficient. If there was a way to value, or rank, these results for the user, Page thought, it would be a great leap forward, a breakthrough in search.

Page thought he could devise a solution, and he decided to make his inquiries the subject of his doctoral dissertation. (A dissertation is a long, scholarly paper or project. Along with the required class work and examinations, it is the major requirement for receiving a doctorate degree in a particular field of study.) Brin was having trouble deciding on a topic for his own dissertation. Among the projects he considered was developing a method to put back together paper documents that had been shredded. He decided to join Page in his work. "I talked to lots of research groups [at Stanford]," Brin says, "and this was the most exciting project."[1]

NOT THE SAME THING

In order to understand Page and Brin's project, one has to know a little bit more about the Internet, the World Wide Web, and how search engines work. Although the term "Internet search" is widely used, what one is really talking about is searching the World Wide Web, or Web. People often use the terms "Internet" and "World Wide Web" interchangeably, but they are not really the same thing.

The Internet is a global network of computers, connected primarily through fiber-optic cables. The number of computers connected in this way is in the millions. The Internet began in the 1950s as a project of the U.S. Defense Department and various universities that worked closely with it. Those connected to the Internet gained the ability to exchange important and sensitive scientific, academic, and research information related to Defense Department projects. Any computer linked to the Internet can communicate with any other computer linked to the network. A variety of computer languages are used to exchange information over the Internet.

The World Wide Web, or Web, is one method of accessing and sharing information on the Internet. Using a computer language called HTML (hypertext markup language) and a protocol, or method of exchanging data, called HTTP (hypertext transfer protocol), the World Wide Web allows the billions of pages on the Web to connect with one another through links. This creates a metaphorical "web" of information.

Software engineers say that the Web is built "on top of the Internet" in the sense that the Web operates over or on the Internet. Not all of

the information available over the Internet is
accessible via the Web. Thus, when one uses
Google or another search engine to conduct an
Internet search, what one is really searching is
the World Wide Web. Likewise, one does not
really "surf" the Internet; one is surfing the Web.

The Web was invented in 1990 by the
British computer scientist Tim Berners-Lee. He
came up with the idea of connecting hypertext

Seen here is a graphic representation of a fiber-optics telecommunications network in the United States. A similar schematic representation of World Wide Web links would be infinitely more complex.

with the Internet and developed a method of doing so. The Web debuted as a public service on the Internet in August 1991. Less than two years later, in April 1993, Berners-Lee and his colleagues announced that the World Wide Web would be a free service. Between 1993 and 1996, the number of Web sites grew from approximately 130 to more than 600,000, making search an increasingly relevant problem.

One accesses specific Web pages either by entering a URL (URL stands for uniform resource locator, a protocol that essentially serves as a site's address on the Web) into the browser or by clicking links on various Web pages. Either method of access, however, requires a key bit of initial information to utilize: the URL of a specific Web page.

Yet what if a person wants to reach a Web page but knows neither the URL of it or any page that links to it? Or what if a person does not know if a Web page on a specific subject even exists, but wants to find out? What if a person wants to find out what information is available on the Web on a specific subject?

HOW A SEARCH ENGINE SEARCHES

What is needed is essentially a card catalog, telephone book, or index to the World Wide Web.

ENQUIRE WITHIN UPON EVERYTHING

While working at CERN, a particle physics laboratory in Geneva, Switzerland, in the 1980s, Tim Berners-Lee, a young British software programmer, became fascinated by the potential of the Internet as a means of large-scale information exchange. What was needed, he realized, was a way of linking together documents that could be easily accessed. This could eliminate the need for any kind of "central management" of this type of information exchange; anyone who wanted to link to the Internet could do so.

Berners-Lee called the first program he created to address this challenge Enquire Within upon Everything, after a children's encyclopedia from his youth. He followed that with the creation of HTML and HTTP, the language and protocol that enabled the linking of documents that in turn made the World Wide Web a reality. With Berners-Lee's invention, the Web truly became something of which users can seemingly inquire within about everything.

Equally important to the Web's growth and development was Berners-Lee's conviction that it should be and should always remain a means of the free exchange of information. Accordingly, Berners-Lee sought no patent or royalties for his invention of the Web. While others have looked for ways to cash in on the growth of the Web, Berners-Lee, as head of the W3 Consortium, continues to dedicate his work to maintaining open access to the Web.

There is no practical way to compile or publish such a document. It would be too bulky and cumbersome for an individual to use. In addition, it would always be going out of date; one of the beautiful things about the Web as a source of information is how easy it is for individuals to add pages to it. The Web grows in size by hundreds, if not thousands, of pages every single day.

Using a search engine, a computer could sift through such information and return results in seconds. Then, as now, search engines all worked in essentially the same basic way. A Web search engine is a sophisticated piece of software, or a computer program. It begins by using another program, called a spider, which "crawls" the Web looking for and retrieving Web pages and documents and feeding them to another program called an indexer. (The spider is also sometimes referred to as a crawler or Web crawler.) Using criteria that have been programmed into it, the indexer "reads" these documents and creates an index of Web pages. This reading is actually a scan, usually for the frequency with which certain specified keywords appear on a site. The more complete and up-to-date the index is, the better results the search engine will return. The

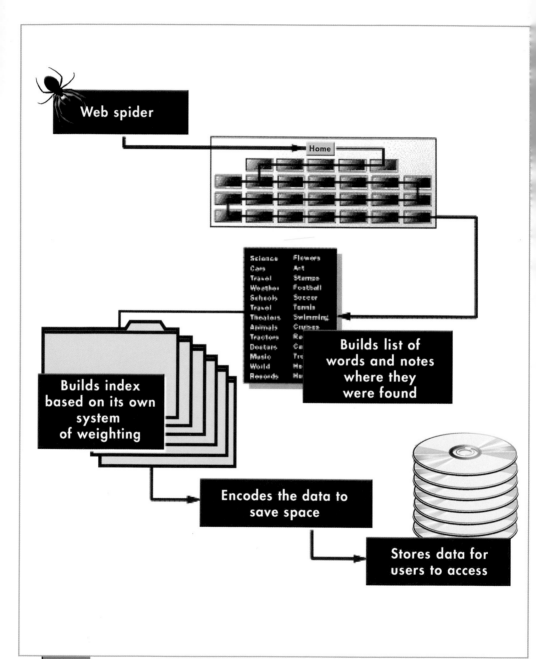

As illustrated here, the fundamental operating principles of a basic search engine are fairly easy to understand.

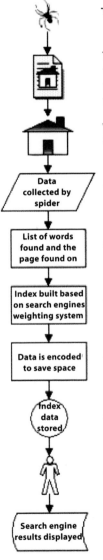

The search engine spider goes out checking web pages.

The search finds the home page of each site found.
- ✓ reads the head section of the page
- ✓ reads the page content
- ✓ finds and follows the links

When the spider has finished it's World Wide check of Web pages, it returns home carrying all the details about your Web site.

Data collected by spider

The search engine's database takes the data collected.

List of words found and the page found on

A list of words found and what page they were found on it built.

Index built based on search engines weighting system

The Web pages are indexed based on the search engine's system of indexing.

Data is encoded to save space

The index data is encoded to save on storage space.

Index data stored

The index data is stored and waits for search engine users to perform a search.

Someone visits the search engine and types in a search word or phrase.

Search engine results displayed

The search engine searches it's data and displays the results.

All search engines share basic operating principles, as outlined in this graphic. What separated Google from its competitors was the criteria for search that Page and Brin incorporated into their algorithm.

HOW A SEARCH ENGINE WORKS: THE BASICS

All search engines, including Google, use the same basic five-step process, as outlined below. It is the refinements that each applies to this process that determine the differences between search engines, especially the variations in the results they return for a specific query.

1. Computer "robots," often referred to as spiders or crawlers, trawl the Web for documents. The information they obtain is gathered in what is known as the search engine's index, which is similar to the index in the back of a book. It tells what pages contain the words for which the spiders have been instructed to search.

2. An individual user types a request for information into the search engine. Such requests are known as queries.

3. The Web server sends the query to the index servers, which provide the name and location of pages that are relevant to the query.

4. The query is then routed to the document servers, which actually retrieve the stored Web pages, or documents. Snippets of those documents are generated to describe each search result to the user.

5. The search results are returned to the user. The entire process takes only a fraction of a second.

search engine's crawl is performed constantly (or as frequently as possible) so that the index is constantly being updated. When a user types a request for a search, the search engine consults the index. It then returns the results to the user in the form of a list of Web pages, with links, URLs, and a brief summary of their contents.

What search engines could not do well, in Page's opinion, was evaluate the information they found in a way that was helpful to the user. The information they returned was essentially, in engineering jargon, undifferentiated. This means the search engine retrieved the information, but it did not sort or evaluate it in a way that Page found meaningful, useful, or effective. Page and Brin's discovery of a way of doing so would be what made Google, Google.

CHAPTER THREE

ACCESSIBLE AND USEFUL

What Page had in mind was the creation of a different kind of algorithm for his prospective search engine. An algorithm is simply a formula or series of steps used to solve a specific problem. While it sounds like it must be a very complicated mathematical term, everyone uses some form of algorithm every day. A recipe for preparing and cooking a favorite food, for example, is a kind of algorithm.

For a computer programmer, the highest form of praise for an algorithm is to say that it is elegant. That means that in terms of the level of complication of the problem it is addressing, the algorithm is simple and requires the fewest number of steps possible.

Page recognized that the essence of the Web was the links that joined its various pages to one another. Every Web site has links, which are words or terms that when clicked on bring the user to another page that the designer of the original site thinks might be of additional use or interest. Such links are usually highlighted in some way on the page and/or listed separately under a heading for "links."

GOING BACK

A visitor to a Web site can easily see what other sites are linked to it. What is not evident is what sites link to it in the same way—the so-called back links. Page believed that analyzing a site's back links could provide a way to rank Web sites. His thinking drew from common practice in the academic world in which he and Brin were pursuing their work. In academia, a primary way of measuring the importance of a specific research paper or work was the number of subsequent research papers that consulted it or otherwise drew on the work therein, even to refute it. A researcher is supposed to list in his or her own work the other papers and works that are consulted in doing that research. That list is known as a paper's citations. A paper that is

Google went from a graduate thesis to becoming one of fastest-growing companies ever. Here, Sergey Brin (left) and Larry Page attend a press conference to promote a new Google service on October 7, 2004. Ironically, Google's founders didn't complete their graduate degree requirements.

frequently cited by other people doing research in the same field is thus assumed to be important or influential. This is in the belief that a lot of other people doing the same kind of work found it useful enough to cite.

Page applied the same logic to Web sites. He reasoned that one way to determine a useful Web page on any given subject was to measure and analyze the number of back links to it. Presumably, one major reason that the creator of a Web site links to another site is because he believes that visitors to his own site would also find something of value and interest on the linked site. One could then apply that same logic to all the sites reached via the back links. A value could be assigned to each back-linked page by determining how many pages, in turn, to which it was back linked, and so on. The program would essentially rank the back links as well. The premise would be that some back links were more valuable—as judged by the number of their back links—than others. By following back links through the Web and ana- lyzing the results, Page believed he could rank the usefulness, as measured by Web users, of any particular Web page.

DEMOCRATIC SEARCH

Simply put, the most useful pages would be the ones with the most back links. Those would be the ones listed first in the results returned to the user of Page and Brin's search engine. Page believed the Web would increase in importance to the extent that it was practical and accessible to users. His proposed method of ranking pages followed naturally from that belief. A given Web page would have a large number of back links because other users had found it useful—practical and accessible—in Page's terms.

As Page saw it, this system had the additional benefit of being essentially neutral or value-free. It did not attempt to reach some kind of independent, critical judgment about the inherent value, worth, or even accuracy of a particular page. It simply measured how useful other Web users had found it to be. In a sense, it let Web users determine for themselves what Web sites were best—that is, useful. Page saw his method as essentially democratic; a link to Web site B by Web site A was essentially a "vote" by Web site A for Web site B. The site with the most votes "won,"showing up at the top of the listings to the searcher. As Google explains it today, the system uses the "collective intelligence of the Web," absent "human involvement or manipulation," to "determine a page's importance."[1] As the number of Web users grew, there would be even more back links, more data, more "votes" to analyze, making the Web, Page and Brin believed, an ever more open and democratic institution.

What Page and Brin now needed was an algorithm that would enable their search engine to perform the necessary analysis of back links. Obviously, the math involved grows incredibly complicated as one follows links back through the Web and assigns values to all the connected pages. With his prodigious mathematical abilities, Brin took the lead in devising the algorithm that would allow their search engine to perform this kind of analysis and prepare its index accordingly. The elegant algorithm that resulted involves more than 500 million variables and 2 billion separate terms.[2] They called it PageRank—both a tribute to its creator and a description of what it does. Eventually, Google's crawl would incorporate PageRank with what it calls Hypertext-Matching Analysis. This is another algorithm that allows its search engine to analyze the full text content of a page using various incorporated criteria rather than just the frequency of certain keywords.

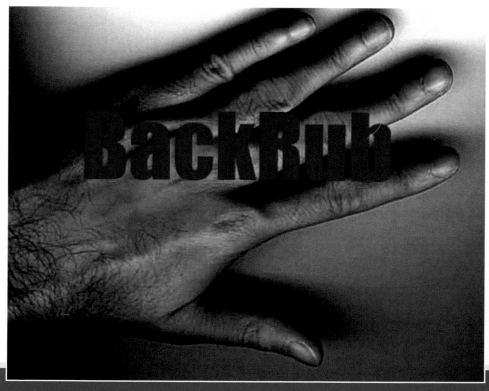

BackRub was the name Brin and Page initially gave to the search engine they developed using an algorithm devised to search back links among Web pages. This was their logo for the program, as it appeared on Web pages maintained by the computer science department at Stanford.

BackRub Becomes Google

At first, Brin and Page called their search engine BackRub (because it depended on the analysis of back links), but as their project grew more ambitious, they began referring to it as "Google." In mathematics, "googol" is the term for the number designated by 1 followed by 100 zeroes. It is a number of almost unimaginable magnitude yet finite extent. For Page and Brin, it symbolized their ambition to use their search engine to "organize the immense amount of information available on the Web."[3]

Their methods were not always as grand as their ambition. With limited financial resources, Page and Brin constantly had to scrounge hardware to use, as well as to beg for space on Stanford's computer network. At times they "borrowed" computers from the university's computer lab and even from the loading dock of the computer science building after deliveries of new equipment. Obviously, in order to crawl the Web, a search engine requires access to an enormous amount of computer memory. For that reason, the pair's search for more machines to add to their network was perpetual. (This

"WE PRESENT GOOGLE"

"The Anatomy of a Large-Scale Hypertextual Web Search Engine" was Brin and Page's formal introduction of Google to the wider world outside the Stanford University computer science program. Right at the outset, the two students were forthright in declaring what they believed they had accomplished with Google:

> In this paper, we present Google, a prototype of a large-scale search engine which makes heavy use of the structure present in hypertext. Google is designed to crawl and index the Web efficiently and produce much more satisfying results than existing systems . . . To engineer a search engine is a challenging task. Search engines index tens to hundreds of millions of web pages involving a comparable number of distinct terms. They answer tens of millions of queries every day. Despite the importance of large-scale search engines on the web, very little academic research has been done on them. Furthermore, due to rapid advance in technology and web proliferation, creating a web search engine today is very different from three years ago. This paper provides an in-depth description of our large-scale web search engine—the first such detailed public description we know of to date.

proved to be something of a blessing in disguise. It demonstrated to them the value of a network of linked smaller computers in opposition to the massive megacomputer that would have been required for all the data storage and memory necessary for their search engine. Accordingly, today Google is driven by the "distributed computing" of some 10,000 linked computers

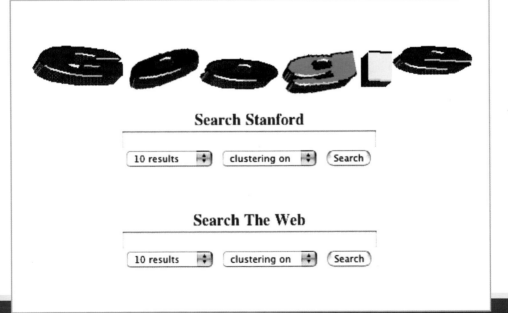

This home page for an early demo of Google, as presented on Stanford University Web pages, already shows the famously uncluttered style that would distinguish Google from competing Web portals.

on its "server farm" rather than massive mainframe machines.)

Though their constant appropriation of space on the university network often brought Brin and Page into conflict with Stanford administrators, repeated testing of Google brought exciting results—quicker, more relevant searches. Fellow students in the program began to use Google and were invariably impressed, as were Stanford faculty members. Word of the project began to circulate among software developers and venture capitalists in Silicon Valley.

A PROJECT BECOMES A BUSINESS

By the beginning of 1998, it was clear that Google had potential as a start-up company. Its two inventors then began to focus on it as more of a business proposition than as a doctoral thesis. Page converted his dorm room at Stanford to Google's "data center," while Brin turned his into the Google "business office." Friends such as David Filo and Jerry Yang, Stanford graduate students who had founded the Internet portal company Yahoo! in 1995, encouraged them (although Filo and Yang were not interested in licensing Google as the search engine for their

THE WORLD'S MOST-VIEWED ARTIST?

Among Google's first employees was Dennis Hwang, who was brought on as an intern at the Googleplex in 2000. Today, although Hwang's name is not well known, the work of this twenty-seven-year-old Korean American computer artist certainly is. Indeed, his art may be viewed by more people, on a daily basis, than that of any other artist in the world.

Since 2000, Hwang has been the designer responsible for the whimsical, humorous modifications to the Google logo that appear on holidays (Valentine's Day, New Year's Day, and so on) and other occasions that are special to the Google founders (the anniversary of the first manned flight, Albert Einstein's birthday, the fiftieth anniversary of the discovery of the double-helix structure of DNA, and the like). Hwang's distinctive work, which is preserved on the Google site (www.google.com/holidaylogos.html), has won him a worldwide following as the "Google doodler."

Dennis Hwang displays one of his sketch designs for the Google home page. The uncluttered simplicity of the Google home page has become a keystone of the company's corporate identity.

portal). Meanwhile, Brin's faculty adviser on his doctoral thesis was telling him, "Look, if this Google thing works out, great. If not, you can return to graduate school and finish your thesis."[4]

Later in 1998, Page and Brin published a short, scholarly paper, "The Anatomy of a Large-Scale Hypertextual Web Search Engine." It explained the PageRank algorithm and their concept for Google. The paper, which has since gone on to "become the most widely cited search-related publication in the world,"[5] only increased the growing hype in the valley about Google.

Brin and Page began actively to seek out financing for Google. They hoped to at least obtain enough to pay off their maxed-out credit cards and move out of the dorms. But this was Silicon Valley, after all, at the height of the great age of Internet start-ups. A faculty member, David Cheriton, arranged for Brin and Page to meet with Andy Bechtolsheim, a founder of Sun Microsystems, a computer and software manufacturer. To the students' chagrin, the busy Bechtolsheim suggested an 8 AM meeting—Brin and Page seldom got up that early—on the porch of Cheriton's house in Palo Alto, which he had to pass on his way to work.

Bechtolsheim watched a quick demonstration of Google, but he was in a hurry and had little time to spend on details. "Instead of us discussing all the details," he asked, "why don't I just write you a check?"[6] He asked Brin and Page how much money they needed, and then wrote out a check to Google for $100,000—twice the amount the two had suggested.

Google was in business. To celebrate, Brin and Page went to Burger King for breakfast—it was accessible and practical. The check was tossed into a desk drawer in Page's dorm room, the Google "data center," where it remained for several weeks. Without a company bank account, the two new search engine entrepreneurs had nowhere to deposit it.

CHAPTER FOUR

THE BETTER MOUSETRAP

Over the next several weeks, Brin and Page concentrated on putting together the necessary paperwork for Google to be incorporated and on finding more financing. They succeeded in raising almost $1 million, mostly from their families, friends, and Silicon Valley connections. On September 7, 1998, Google was officially incorporated, with Page listed as chief executive officer (CEO) and Brin as president. The company's first office space was the garage of a friend's house in Menlo Park, a suburb of Palo Alto.

By the end of the year the search engine was answering 10,000 search queries a day. The company had also received the first of what would be years of adoring notices in the press, having received glowing profiles in *Time* magazine

The Google campus, as the company likes to refer to its corporate headquarters in Mountain View, California, is also known as the Googleplex. This is a photograph of the entrance there on October 20, 2005, one day before the company's stock price reached an all-time high.

and *USA Today*. In December, *PC Magazine* named Google one of its top 100 Web sites and search engines for 1998.

THE GOOGLEPLEX

By the spring of 1999, the company was up to ten employees (besides the two founders) and was renting more formal office space in Palo Alto. More important, the search engine was successfully handling more than 500,000 search queries per day. In June, Brin and Page announced that they had succeeded in raising more than $25 million in financing from Silicon Valley's two top venture capital firms. Among other things, the money financed Google's move to a huge new office space in Mountain View, the soon-to-be legendary Googleplex, which it still occupies. The company now had thirty-nine employees, and the search engine performed 3 million Web searches per day.

The corporate culture that developed at the Googleplex was typical of many of the Internet start-ups in the valley at the time, simultaneously relaxed and hard-driven. The main workspace was open, without cubicles or walls. Wooden doors laid across sawhorses served as desks, on top of which were perched

At the Googleplex, employees are provided with all manners of relaxation, recreation, and entertainment, in the belief that such benefits spur creativity and loyalty and make the long hours required of employees more palatable. Here, an employee relaxes at a piano in the company game room, which also features video games and recreation balls along with a myriad of other "toys."

state-of-the-art computers. Large rubber exercise balls served as avant-garde chairs, decoration, and toys for when employees need a moment to relax or blow off steam. Employees were allowed to bring pets to work, and several dogs regularly roamed the Googleplex. Under the direction of a chef who formerly cooked for the rock band the Grateful Dead, the cafeteria served a full menu of innovative, healthful meals around the clock, at no cost to the employees. Lava lamps became the lighting of choice.

Salaries were low, particularly for graduates of top-flight engineering schools such as Stanford. The hours were long, but the people who worked at Google were savvy enough about the way Silicon Valley worked to expect a future reward for their hard work and sacrifices in the present. Although rarely discussed openly, it was generally assumed that at some point in the not-too-distant future, Google would go public—offer its stock for sale to investors. Already, there had been speculation in the press about when an initial public offering might take place. Such IPOs are the pot of gold at the end of the Silicon Valley rainbow. When the company is ready to go public, employees are customarily compensated with shares of company stock as reward for their service in laying the foundation of the company's success. If all goes well with the IPO, as it has with so many Silicon Valley start-ups, Google would have suddenly become a company of millionaires.

Brin and Page's time at Stanford coincided with the opening of the Gates Computer Science Building as the home of the university's computer science department and a computer laboratory. The building was named for William "Bill" Gates, the founder of Microsoft. Gates is one of the few great American high-tech successes who did not start out in Silicon Valley.

THE COMPANY EVERYONE LOVES

Success followed success, and Google continued to grow. By the middle of 2000, Google was handling 18 million search queries per day. Its search engine index had more than 1 billion Web documents in it. By the end of the year, the number of daily search requests on Google exceeded 100 million.

Search the web using Google!

(Google Search) (I'm feeling lucky)

Special Searches	Help!	Get Google! updates monthly:
Stanford Search	About Google!	
Linux Search	Company Info	your e-mail
	Google! Logos	(Subscribe) Archive

Copyright ©1998 Google Inc.

Although this is a prototype Google home page from a demo developed while Brin and Page were still at Stanford, it is nonetheless instantly recognizable to current users.

Meanwhile, the press continued to rave about Google, making advertising unnecessary. Each new rave article did Google's advertising for it, for free. The famously uncluttered Google home page, with its exceedingly few words and sometimes whimsical illustrations, became a pop-culture icon. Although Brin and Page claim the clean look of the home page is a happy accident that came about because "we're not Web designers and [we] don't do HTML,"[1] they recognize what they have and are fanatical about limiting the number of words that appear on its page. The design seems to symbolize what users like about using Google itself—it is unpretentious, free of hype, easy to look at and use, and practical and accessible. The approach seems even to extend to Page and Brin's attitude toward any kind of personal publicity, which they shun. At the same time that Google was being extolled in the press, very little was ever written or known about the personal lives of Brin and Page.

Google, it seemed, was the company everyone loved. Page and Brin created a better mousetrap, and the whole world seemed to clamor for it. There was just one problem. Brin and Page had not yet figured out a way to turn the widespread desire for their product into a profitable business.

THE SPIRIT OF THE TIMES

"Zeitgeist" is a German word that means the general intellectual, moral, and cultural climate of an era, or the spirit of the times. With its ability to track what people are interested in at any given moment, as indicated by what topics they are searching for information about, Google is able to provide its own insight into the spirit of the times.

The Google Zeitgeist (http://www.google.com/press/zeitgeist.html) is Google's analysis of various trends and patterns evident in its search statistics. Essentially, it is a record of the most popular search queries in a variety of categories over time. It includes what queries are gaining the most in popularity at a given time, and what queries are declining at the same time. By looking at the Google Zeitgeist for a particular week or month, one gets a glimpse of what topics, subjects, people, and events were on the minds of Google users at that time. This provides a simultaneous portrait, perhaps, of what is going on in the world at that particular time.

For example, if one looks at the Google Zeitgest archive for August 2001, one gets a picture of an America largely unconcerned with anything too "serious," one preoccupied with celebrities and amusing itself. Of the "Top 10 Gaining Queries" for that month, three were celebrities—the recently deceased R & B singer Aaliyah, troubled pop siren Mariah Carey, and actress Shannon Elizabeth, who starred in movies such as *American Pie* and *Tomcats*. Two others were sports-related—fantasy football and the PGA championship. A sixth embraced celebrity and sports, especially Lisa Harrison, who had just been designated *Playboy* magazine's sexiest basketball player in the WNBA. Another was the multistate lottery Powerball. The remaining three—Baycol, a recently recalled cholesterol drug; the CodeRed computer virus; and Zone Alarm computer firewall technology—showed that Americans had something on their minds besides pop culture, sports, and gambling, but they hardly constituted an ominous portent for the future.

A month later, things were very different. A simple listing of the "Top 10 Gaining Queries" for September 2001 tells another story. From top to bottom, they were: Nostradamus; CNN; World Trade Center; Osama bin Laden; Taliban; Afghanistan; NIMDA (a computer virus); American flag; BBC; and FBI. What had happened to change the zeitgeist so radically, of course, was the September 11 terrorist attacks by Al Qaeda on the World Trade Center in New York City and the Pentagon in Washington, D.C.

The company had plenty of money—almost $20 million from the financiers—but its operating expenses were more than $500,000 a month and steadily increased as the company continued to expand to meet user demand. At that rate, with no reliable form of revenue, Google would soon run out of money.

DOOMED START-UPS

It was becoming an all too common—and sad—
story in Silicon Valley and among NASDAQ
investors. (The NASDAQ is the electronic stock
market where the shares in most Internet start-up
companies—also called "dot-coms" for the common suffix in their URL—were traded.) By March
2000, the mania for Internet stocks had driven
their prices to an all-time high on the NASDAQ.
That year, there were 457 IPOs, most of them in
Internet stocks. Of those, 117 doubled in price on
the first day of trading.[2] But the bubble was about
to burst, as investors began to realize that very
few of the dot-coms had viable plans for turning a
revenue. Most had financed themselves through
infusions of cash from venture capitalists and
IPOs. They essentially gave their products or services away in the hopes of building consumer
demand while they figured out a way to make
money from what they did. Between March 11,
2000, and October 9, 2002, Internet stocks on
the NASDAQ lost 78 percent of their value. The
boom in Internet stocks that had fueled so much
of the rampant economic growth of the U.S.
economy in the late 1990s came to be seen as
hype, at best, and a swindle or fraud at worst.

Although it had not yet offered its stock for sale, in some ways Google seemed no different from many of these doomed start-ups. It had an exciting, cutting-edge product that worked and that people loved, but seemingly no way to make money from it. It cost nothing to use the Google search engine. Users were not about to start paying to use the service, even if Brin and Page had wanted to charge them. After all, libraries do not charge for card catalog use, and telephone books are free. With a service that was so popular and worked so well, Brin and Page obviously did not want to do anything that would drastically change their users' experience. After all, it was in Page and Brin's ultimate interest to increase the number of users of the Web, not to make it more difficult for them to find information on it.

MIND-SPACE

What Google did have, however, as Brin and Page quickly realized, was users. Google had a truly enormous number of users, accustomed to using Google frequently, if not daily, and devoted to the service. And there was the answer. Google would not and could not charge users for access to its search engine. However, it did have a group that it could charge, in essence, for access to its

WATCH WHERE YOU'RE LOOKING

Google's rise to profitability in 2001 enabled it to acquire and develop a whole new range of products beyond its basic search engine. The full list of these tools and services can be seen by clicking on "more" on the Google home page. The list includes Google News, Google Images (which allows you to search an immense data bank of photos and visual images related to a particular search query), Froogle (a guide to shopping over the Internet), and Google Maps, which provides interactive maps and satellite imagery for virtually any location in the world.

In the summer of 2005, a new product, Google Earth, offered viewers what Google called a "three-dimensional" guide to the world, a "globe inside your computer." Combining satellite technology with state-of-the-art mapping, Google Earth allows users to access satellite photographs of virtually any location on the planet, with individual focus as near as an individual building.

Although the *New York Times* praised Google Earth as the ultimate product for anyone "who ever dreamed of flying," others were not as impressed. Many concerned citizens and politicians across the United States expressed worry that the services could be used by terrorists to access and research potential targets.

users, in a way that would minimally affect users' experience with Google.

Who was that group? Advertisers.

Advertisers pay for space, for access to places

where people are likely to see or hear their advertisements. These include billboards, the sides of buildings and buses, commercials during television programs, magazines and newspapers, or voice-over spots on the radio. It is probably safe to say that just about anywhere a person might see an advertisement, an advertiser would pay to put it there, provided the price was right. That price is determined by how many people are likely to see the advertisement in any given place. The more people who are likely to see it, the higher the price the advertiser is likely to be willing to pay for the space. That is why, for example, advertisers are typically charged the highest rates to place commercials during the most-watched television programs.

The type of viewer who might see their advertisement is almost equally important for advertisers. Advertising in the United States is a multibillion dollar industry whose practitioners like to think of it as a science. An advertiser wants as much information as is possible about the people who are likely to be exposed to an advertisement in a given place. Advertisers do not want to know just how many people read a certain magazine, for example. They want to know how old those readers are likely to be, their sex, their race or ethnic background, what they do for a living, how much money they make, where they live, and what their attitudes are about certain topics. The more information like this an advertiser has, the better chance it has of placing an advertisement where it will likely be seen by someone with a probable interest in the product being advertised. Such information allows advertisers to better target those who see, hear, look at, or read its advertisements. And every viewer, every listener, and every reader is a potential customer.

What Google had to offer advertisers was not just users, but targeted users. In theory, every single search inquiry, more than 100 million a day by the end of 2000, could provide an advertiser with a piece of information about the user that it would have been previously impossible for that advertiser to obtain. Moreover, that particular piece of information was arguably the single most important thing that an advertiser could ever want to know. That piece of information was immediate, almost instantaneous access to a potential customer's mind.

CHAPTER FIVE

GOING PUBLIC

Think about it. You own or run a company that makes guitars, or a music store that sells guitars. You want to advertise your product, and obviously you want your advertisements to be as effective as possible. What could be more potentially effective than placing your advertisement in a space where you can be certain that it will be seen by the viewer at the precise instant that he or she is thinking about guitars?

This is what Brin and Page ultimately realized they had available to offer to advertisers. Beginning in 2001, Google enabled advertisers to bid on certain key words. These key words, however, were not in the text of the Web page, but were possible terms a user of the Google search engine might enter into the search box when

Google corporate officials, including chief executive officer Eric Schmidt *(second from left)* and founder Larry Page *(center)*, celebrate as Google is listed for the first time as a publicly traded company on the NASDAQ stock exchange.

making a search inquiry (the word "guitar," for example). When Google returned its results for its Web search on guitar, it would also return, on the right-hand side of the page, a short list of advertisements from guitar manufacturers and sellers—those who had bid the highest for the right to advertise on the keyword "guitar." The highest bidder would have its advertisement listed first. Per Google policy, the advertisements had to be identical in design and form—simple, unobtrusive four-line notices, without graphics. They usually included a brief heading, followed by two lines of simple description and summary, and the URL on the last line.

INSTANT ACCESS

The attraction for the advertiser was obvious. At the exact moment that a person was interested enough in guitars that he or she was looking up information on them—which made them, in the advertiser's mind, a potential customer—that person would be shown the advertiser's ad for guitars. Advertisers could capitalize on consumer interest in a way that could not be achieved, for example, even by placing an advertisement in a music magazine. There was, after all, no guarantee that the purchaser of the magazine was interested in guitars, as opposed to other musical instruments. Even if the magazine was specifically devoted only to guitars, there was no guarantee that the person who bought it would ever look at it, or read it all the way through.

Google further refined this new program, which it called AdWords, by rewarding those advertisers whose ads did the best. Using an algorithm similar to that of PageRank, Google measured the value or effectiveness of such advertisements by recording how many users linked to each one by clicking on it. Over time, an advertiser with more "clickthroughs" might be moved higher in the listings than one who had bid more for the keyword. An advertisement that received too few clickthroughs could be moved down or even dropped. Brin and Page's logic was that the number of clickthroughs reflected the collective judgment of Google users as to the usefulness of a particular advertisement, just as its PageRank algorithm back links measured the value of a Web site. For this reason, AdWords is sometimes referred to as AdRank.

AdWords was a success with both advertisers and Google users. Advertisers found that, overall, the program gave them a better return

WANT A COOKIE?

Google is not without its critics, whose numbers rise as the company grows more powerful. The most serious criticism involves Google's potential for privacy abuses. Each time a person uses Google, the company plants what is known as a "cookie" on their hard drive. A cookie is a piece of computer programming allowing Google to record everywhere the user goes on the Web. This includes any information a visitor provides a site, such as phone numbers, Social Security number, addresses, bank account numbers, credit card numbers, and so forth.

Although Google maintains that it has safeguards in place to protect such information, the potential for abuse is great. Especially worrisome is the possibility that Google might be compelled to turn such information over to the government.

The pressure that a government could exert on Google was illustrated in late 2005, when Google revealed that it had reached an agreement to provide its service to the more than one billion citizens of the People's Republic of China. But to do so, Google has agreed to provide only those search results approved by the Chinese government. For example, Chinese users of Google searching for information on controversial events in Chinese history, such as the massacre of hundreds of pro-democracy protestors by the Chinese government in Tiananmen Square in Beijing in 1989, will only receive results approved by `that government. Critics point out that such arrangements are directly contrary to the goal of keeping the Web a conduit for the free flow of information, and of providing unbiased, "democratic" search results.

Google CEO Eric Schmidt (standing) poses with the company's founders Brin (left) and Page. Despite Schmidt's title, and Brin and Page's retreat into more of a background role, Google insiders generally maintain that all major corporate decisions are still made by the founders.

on their advertising investment than older, more conventional means of advertising. Some users complained that AdWords contributed to the growing commercialization of the Web, a development that they found unwelcome. However, most Google users did not seem to object. This may have been, in large part, because a majority of searchers were coming to use the Web for commercial purposes—to shop for, buy, or sell goods and services. In this sense, the advertisements were likely seen as being more of a source of potential information than any kind of unwanted commercial intrusion.

In "The Anatomy of a Large-Scale Hypertextual Web Search Engine," Page and Brin had essentially dismissed the idea of advertising on Google. "The goals of the advertising business model do not always correspond to providing quality search to users," they wrote. ". . . We believe the issue of advertising causes enough mixed incentives that it is crucial to have a competitive search engine that is transparent," that is, free of advertising.[1] But that paper had been written when Google was still nothing more than a graduate school project. Now, it was a big business, growing bigger every day.

TURNING A PROFIT

It was advertising revenue that would fuel that continued growth. In the last quarter of 2001, Google turned a profit for the first time, which

An entry of the word "computers" into the Google search engine indicates how its advertising program works for a basic search. The three companies listed at top, in the shaded region, are labeled "Sponsored Links," meaning that they have paid for the privilege of appearing there. The listings below are those returned by the Google PageRank algorithm. At right appear the brief simple advertisements of the companies that have bid the highest on the key word "computers."

A DIFFERENT KIND OF COMPANY

When a company first intends to offer its stock for sale, it has to file a public document, known as an S1, with the Securities and Exchange Commission (SEC), the federal government agency responsible for regulating the nation's stock markets. Among other things, the S1 contains relevant financial information about the company, intended to allow potential investors to assess its business prospects. The S1 also contains, for similar reasons, a statement of the company's business and management philosophies and practices.

Google's statement in its S1 was as unusual as the company itself. In what it called "Letter from the Founders: An Owner's Manual for Google's Shareholders," Page advised future investors that "Google is not a conventional company" and that "We do not intend to become one." Google had been managed "differently," Page asserted, and it would continue to be managed differently even under public ownership. The main management difference, Page made clear, was that he and Brin (and to a lesser extent CEO Eric Schmidt) would continue to make all the major decisions, with their view of what Google should be, not the wishes of its shareholders, being the most important factor.

Although many Wall Street analysts condemned the statement as "arrogant," investors did not seem to mind at the time of the IPO or afterward. Indeed, in the first week of October 2005, some fourteen months after the IPO, Google stock was selling at its highest price ever—more than $320 a share.

allowed it to introduce new services. One of these services uses Google's search algorithms to create a continuously updated Web news site, Google News, by constantly crawling 4,000 online news services. Google boasts that Google News is "the first ever news service compiled solely by computer algorithms without human intervention."[2]

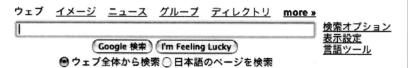

This is Google's home page as it appears in Japanese. Google features more than 110 different language interfaces, from Afrikaans to Zulu.

That same year, Brin and Page hired Eric Schmidt, a longtime Silicon Valley executive, as CEO of Google. The move was widely seen as a means of assuring prospective stock market investors that the company had an experienced business executive at the helm. For all of their genius and success, both Page and Brin were still younger than thirty years old, with no experience running a company. Also, the bursting of the dot-com bubble had left investors somewhat wary of all the young Internet hotshots from Silicon Valley. Although Brin and Page assumed new titles—Brin as president of technology, Page as president of products—by most accounts they continued to make all the important decisions pertaining to the company.

Over the next three years, Google continued to grow at a phenomenal rate, posting annual revenue increases of more than 100 percent, increasing the number of Web pages in its index to more than eight billion, and raising the number of its employees to more than 2,000. Google created Web domains in more than 100 languages, making its user interface available in more than 100 languages besides English. Numerous new services for individual users were developed,

adding a slew of impressive corporate clients
(the *New York Times*, the Central Intelligence
Agency, Yahoo!, to name just a few) who wish
to use Google search technology in their own
businesses, and otherwise paving the way for the
inevitable IPO.

A video screen at the Nasdaq MarketSite in New York City on
August 19, 2004, the first day of Google's initial public offering,
relays the good news: Google's shares are up 17.6 percent in
the early hours of trading.

When at last it came, on August 19, 2004, it was more successful than perhaps anyone besides Sergey Brin and Larry Page could have imagined. The initial asking price for a share of Google stock was $85; by the end of the first day of trading that price had risen to more than $100. By November it was above $200; for much of the summer of 2005 it sold for more than $300. Besides making billionaires of Page and Brin, the offering raised almost $3 billion in working capital for Google. In August 2005, a second offering raised an additional $4 billion in capital.

Incredibly, to the amazement of even the most experienced stock market analysts, Google shares continued to rise. By early 2006, a single share of Google stock was selling for well more than $400. Conservative analysts predicted that Google shares would ultimately peak at between $600 and $700 a share, although one well-regarded broker hazarded that Google shares would not stop rising until the share price exceeded $2,000. Forecasts aside, on January 24, 2006, Google passed Intel and IBM to become the world's second most valuable technology company, after Microsoft. Google now has more than 6,000 employees.

The success of these offerings led to intense speculation as to what Google intended to do

Sitting pretty: The troika of Google—Schmidt *(left)*, Brin *(top)*, and Page—enjoy a brief moment of horseplay before returning to work in this photograph taken on January 15, 2004.

with all that cash. If they know, Brin and Page are not saying. Google's official corporate mission remains what it has been throughout its short, dynamic history: "To organize the world's information and make it universally accessible and useful."[3]

TIMELINE

1939— Stanford graduates Bill Hewlett and Dave Packard found Hewlett-Packard in Palo Alto, California. The company is the first high-tech company in what will become known as Silicon Valley not dependent on U.S. government contracts.

1951— Stanford professor Frederick Terman persuades the university to convert some of its property into the Stanford Research Park, one of the country's first "technology incubators."

1956— Nobel Prize–winning physicist William Shockley opens the Shockley Semiconductor Laboratory in Mountain View, giving increased scientific prestige to Silicon Valley.

1972— Journalist Don Hoefler coins the term "Silicon Valley" to refer to the region of high concentration of semiconductor and

(continued on following page)

TIMELINE

(continued from previous page)

computer-related industries south of San Francisco.

1976— Steve Jobs, Steve Wozniak, and Mike Markkula formally found Apple Computer.

1980— Initial public offering of Apple stock is the most successful in the United States since Ford's in 1956. This heralds the personal computer revolution.

March 1995— Sergey Brin and Larry Page meet during a spring visit organized for prospective computer science graduate students at Stanford.

August 1995— Spectacularly successful IPO of Netscape initiates the boom in dot-com and Internet stocks.

September 1995— Page begins studies at Stanford, where Brin is in his second year in the doctoral program.

January 1996— Brin and Page begin working together on BackRub, a research project intended to produce better search results by analyzing back links on the Web.

1998— BackRub metamorphoses into plans for the Google search engine.

Summer 1998— Brin and Page publish "The Anatomy of a Large-Scale Hypertextual Web Search Engine," a scholarly paper explaining PageRank algorithm and their plans for the Google search engine.

September 1998— Google is officially incorporated.

1999— Page and Brin open Google's Mountain View headquarters, the "Googleplex."

2001— Brin and Page introduce AdWords, Google's targeted advertising program, which assures the company a viable revenue stream and results in immediate profitability.

July 2001— Eric Schmidt is appointed CEO of Google.

(continued on following page)

TIMELINE

(continued from previous page)

2002— Google brings to market Google News, the first-ever news service composed solely by computer algorithms.

August 2004— Google IPO raises billions of dollars in capital for the company.

August 2005— Second stock offering raises additional billions; net worth of Page and Brin is estimated at $11 billion each, placing them at number sixteen on *Forbes* magazine's annual list of the 400 wealthiest Americans under the age of forty.

GLOSSARY

algorithm A formula or series of specific steps for solving a particular problem.

avowal A public acknowledgement or declaration.

capital A stock of accumulated goods or money.

domain A group of computers and devices on a network that are administered as a single unit with common rules and procedures.

dot-coms Companies whose products or services deal with or are sold on the Internet.

entrepreneur One who founds, organizes, and manages a business and assumes its risk.

hardware The physical pieces and components of a computer, such as the keyboard and display screen.

high-tech Short for high technology; refers to technology or a type of technological development that is the most advanced currently available.

initial public offering (IPO) A company's first sale of stock to the public.

interface The place where two independent systems meet, act on, or communicate with each other; in a computer system, for example, the keyboard, mouse, and menus are referred to as the user interface, as they allow the user to communicate with the computer operating system.

Internet A worldwide network of computers linked for the purpose of exchanging information.

portal A Web site or service, such as Yahoo! or AOL, that offers access to the Web along with an array of other services and resources.

search engine A program that searches documents for keywords and provides a list of documents where those words are found; this term is usually used for programs that enable users to find documents on the Web.

server A computer on a network that manages the network resources.

software Computer instructions or data; anything that can be stored electronically on a computer.

speculation The buying or selling of stock in the hope of profiting from a change in its price.

stock market bubble A situation in which stocks are overvalued and their prices rise dramatically because of public or investor enthusiasm.

ubiquitous Widespread; to be everywhere at once.

venture capital Financing for new businesses.

Web browser A computer program, such as Netscape Navigator or Internet Explorer, that is used to locate and display Web pages.

World Wide Web (WWW) A method of exchanging information on the Internet; consists of billions of Web sites or pages with the ability to link to one another and be accessed by individual users.

zeitgeist The general intellectual, moral, and spiritual climate of an era; the spirit of the times.

FOR MORE INFORMATION

Computer History Museum
1401 N. Shoreline Boulevard
Mountain View, CA 94043
(650) 810-1010
Web site: http://www.computerhistory.org

Google Headquarters
1600 Amphitheatre Pkwy
Mountain View, CA 94043
Web site: http://www.google.com/jobs/
   students.html

The NASDAQ Stock Market
One Liberty Plaza
165 Broadway
New York, NY 10006

Stanford Visitor Information Services
551 Serra Mall, Memorial Auditorium Lobby
Stanford, CA 94305-5005
(650) 723-2560
Web site: http://www.stanford.edu/dept/
   visitorinfo/contact/index.html

WEB SITES

Due to the changing nature of Internet links, the Rosen Publishing Group, Inc., has developed an online list of Web sites related to the subject of this book. This site is updated regularly. Please use the link below to access the list:

http://www.rosenlinks.com/icb/sblp

FOR FURTHER READING

Battelle, John. *The Search: How Google and Its Rivals Rewrote the Rules of Business and Transformed Our Culture*. New York, NY: Portfolio, 2005.

Bronson, Po. *The Nudist on the Late Shift and Other True Tales of Silicon Valley*. New York, NY: Broadway, 2000.

Cassidy, John. *Dot.Con: How America Lost Its Mind and Money in the Internet Era*. New York, NY: Perennial, 2003.

Hertzfeld, Andy. *Revolution in the Valley*. Sebastapol, CA: O'Reilly, 2004.

Kaplan, David. *The Silicon Boys and Their Valley of Dreams*. New York, NY: Harper, 2000.

Kaplan, Jerry. *Startup: A Silicon Valley Adventure*. New York, NY: Penguin, 1996.

Kidder, Tracy. *The Soul of a New Machine*. New York, NY: Harper, 1990.

Laing, Gordon. *Digital Retro: The Evolution and Design of the Personal Computer*. San Francisco, CA: Sybex, 2005.

Lewis, Michael. *The New New Thing: A Silicon Valley Story*. New York, NY: Norton, 1999.

Lewis, Michael. *Next: The Future Just Happened.*
New York, NY: Norton, 2001.

Markoff, John. *What the Dormouse Said: How the
60s Counterculture Shaped the Personal
Computer.* New York, NY: Viking, 2005.

Young, Jeffrey. *iCon: Steve Jobs: The Greatest
Second Act in the History of Business.* New York,
NY: John Wiley, 2005.

BIBLIOGRAPHY

Battelle, John. *The Search: How Google and Its Rivals Rewrote the Rules of Business and Transformed Our Culture.* New York, NY: Portfolio, 2005.

Bronson, Po. *The Nudist on the Late Shift and Other True Tales of Silicon Valley.* New York, NY: Broadway, 2000.

Cassidy, John. *Dot.Con: How America Lost Its Mind and Money in the Internet Era.* New York, NY: Perennial, 2003.

Cassidy, Mike. "His Art for Search Engine is Among Most Widely Viewed in the World." MercuryNews.com, April 27, 2004. Retrieved June 21, 2005 (http://www.mercurynews.com/p/articles/mi_kmtmn/is_200404).

"The Complete Guide to Googlemania." *Wired*, March 2004. Retrieved April 26, 2005 (http://www.wired.com/wired/archive/12.03/google.html).

Derbyshire, John. "The Age of Google." *National Review* Online, November 14, 2002. Retrieved June 21, 2005 (http://www.nationalreview.com/derbyshire/derbyshire111403.asp).

Dizard, Wilson P., III. "Intelligence Networks Go for Google." *Government Computer News*, December 5, 2003. Retrieved June 22, 2005 (http://www.gcn.com/vol1_no1/daily-updates/24358-1.html).

Graham, Jefferson. "The Search Engine That Could." *USA Today*, August 25, 2003. Retrieved June 21, 2005 (http://www.usatoday.com/tech/news/2003-08-25-google_x.htm).

Hammonds, Keith. "How Google Grows . . . and Grows . . . and Grows." Fast Company, April 2003. Retrieved June 22, 2005 (http://www.fastcompany.com/magazine/69/google.html).

Hansell, Saul. "All the News Algorithms Fit to Print." *New York Times*, September 24, 2002. Retrieved June 21, 2005 (http://www.nytimes.com/2002/09/24/technology).

Hardy, Quentin. "All Eyes on Google." *Forbes*, May 26, 2003. Retrieved June 21, 2005 (http://www.forbes.com/technology/free_forbes/2003/0526/100.html).

Hertzfeld, Andy. *Revolution in the Valley*. Sebastapol, CA: O'Reilly, 2004.

Kaplan, David. *The Silicon Boys and Their Valley of Dreams*. New York, NY: Harper, 2000.

Kaplan, Jerry. *Startup: A Silicon Valley Adventure.* New York, NY: Penguin, 1996.

Kidder, Tracy. *The Soul of a New Machine.* New York, NY: Harper, 1990.

Laing, Gordon. *Digital Retro: The Evolution and Design of the Personal Computer.* San Francisco, CA: Sybex, 2005.

La Monica, Paul. "Google Sets $2.7 Billion IPO." CNN/Money, April 29, 2004. Retrieved June 25, 2005 (http://www.money.cnn.com/2004/04/29/technology/google).

Lecuyer, Christophe. "Technology and Entrepreneurship in Silicon Valley." Nobelprize.org, December 7, 2004. Retrieved September 20, 2005 (http://www.nobelprize.org/physics/articles/lecuyer).

Lee, Jennifer. "Postcards from Planet Google." *New York Times*, November 28, 2002. Retrieved June 21, 2005 (http://www.nytimes.com/2002/11/28/technology/circuits).

Lewis, Michael. *The New New Thing: A Silicon Valley Story.* New York, NY: Norton, 1999.

Lewis, Michael. *Next: The Future Just Happened.* New York, NY: Norton, 2001.

Liedtke, Michael. "Google Boosts 'Blogging' with New Specialty Search Engine."

SignOnSanDiego.com, September 14, 2005. Retrieved September 14, 2005 (http://www. signonsandiego.com/news/computing/ 20050914-1358-googleblogs.html).

Markoff, John. "In Searching the Web, Google Finds Riches." *New York Times*, April 13, 2003. Retrieved June 21, 2005 (http:// www.nytimes.com/2003/04/13/technology).

Markoff, John. *What the Dormouse Said: How the 60s Counterculture Shaped the Personal Computer*. New York, NY: Viking, 2005.

Naraine, Ryan. "All the News That's Fit to Google." Atnewyork.com, August 6, 2002. Retrieved June 21, 2005 (http://www.atnewyork.com/news/print/ php/1440431).

Patsuris, Penelope. "The Making of a $2 Billion Brand." *Forbes*, February 21, 2003. Retrieved June 21, 2005 (http://www.forbes.com/2003/02/ 21/cx_pp_0221google.html).

Raphael, Todd. "At Google, the Proof Is in the People." *Workforce*, March 2003. Retrieved June 21, 2005 (http://www.workforce.com/ section/09?feature/23/41/03/index.html).

Sherman, Chris. "Happy Birthday, Google!" Search Engine Watch, September 8, 2003. Retrieved

June 22, 2005 (http://www.searchenginewatch.com/searchday/article.php/2160731).

Sherman, Chris. "The Technology Behind Google." Search Engine Watch, August 12, 2002. Retrieved June 22, 2005 (http://www.searchenginewatch.com/searchday/02/sd0812-googletech.html).

Stross, Randall. "What's Google's Secret Weapon? An Army of Ph.D.'s" *New York Times*, June 6, 2004. Retrieved June 21, 2005 (http://www.nytimes.com/2004/06/06/business/yourmoney).

Swisher, Kara. "Beneath Google's Dot-Com Shell, A Serious Player." *Wall Street Journal*, January 21, 2002. Retrieved June 21, 2005 (http://www.online.wsj.com/article/0,SB1013390943280113320.djm).

Ulanoff, Lance. "I Search, Therefore I Google." *PC Magazine*, November 26, 2003. Retrieved June 21, 2005 (http://www.pcmag.com/article2/0,4149,1397999,00.asp).

Young, Jeffrey. *iCon: Steve Jobs: The Greatest Second Act in the History of Business.* New York, NY: John Wiley, 2005.

Source Notes

Introduction

1. John Battelle, *The Search: How Google and Its Rivals Rewrote the Rules of Business and Transformed Our Culture* (New York, NY: Portfolio, 2005), p. 234.
2. Vanity Fair.com. Retrieved September 10, 2005 (http://www.vanityfair.com).

Chapter One

1. Gregory Gromov. NetValley. "Don Hoefler." Retrieved September 4, 2005 (http://www.netvalley.com/donhoefler).
2. Ibid.
3. Dawn Levy. Stanford University News Service. "William Shockley: Still Controversial, After All These Years." October 22, 2002. Retrieved September 4, 2005 (http://stanford.edu/dept/news/pr/02/shockley).
4. "Frederick Terman." Wikipedia. Retrieved September 4, 2005 (http://en.wikipedia.org/).
5. John Battelle, *The Search: How Google and Its Rivals Rewrote the Rules of Business and*

Transformed Our Culture (New York, NY: Portfolio, 2005), pp. 67–68.

6. Google. "Google Corporate Information." Retrieved April 26, 2005 (http://www.google.com/corporate).

7. Battelle, pp. 67–68.

8. Battelle, p. 68.

9. Battelle, p. 66.

CHAPTER TWO

1. John Battelle, *The Search: How Google and Its Rivals Rewrote the Rules of Business and Transformed Our Culture* (New York, NY: Portfolio, 2005), p. 73.

CHAPTER THREE

1. Google. "Google Corporate Information." Retrieved April 26, 2005 (http://www.google.com/corporate).

2. Ibid.

3. Ibid.

4. John Battelle, *The Search: How Google and Its Rivals Rewrote the Rules of Business and Transformed Our Culture* (New York, NY: Portfolio, 2005), p. 82.

5. Ibid., p. 82

6. Google. "Google Corporate Information." Retrieved April 26, 2005 (http://www.google.com/corporate).

Chapter Four

1. Andrew Goodman. Traffick.com. "Google's Endless Summer." Retrieved June 21, 2005 (http://www.traffick.com).

2. Investopedia.com. "Greatest Market Crashes." Retrieved September 20, 2005 (http://investopedia.com/features/crashes).

Chapter Five

1. Sergey Brin and Larry Page, "The Anatomy of a Large-Scale Hypertextual Web Search Engine." Retrieved September 20, 2005 (http: //www.db.stanford.edu/~backrub/google.html).

2. Google. "Google Corporate Information." Retrieved April 26, 2005 (http://www.google.com/corporate).

3. Ibid.

Index

ABOUT THE AUTHOR

Casey White, the author of *John Jay: Diplomat of the American Experiment* in Rosen Publishing's The Library of American Thinkers series, grew up "virtually in the shadow" of the John Jay estate in Katonah, New York, which she credits with inspiring her lifelong interest in this now routinely forgotten founding father. A teacher of American history, White is fascinated by the transformative power of the Internet and related technology on her students, believing that tools such as Google offer the youth of today unprecedented access to whole new worlds of information.

PHOTO CREDITS